296.444
G21   Gaster, Moses.
            The Ketubah.

DATE	ISSUED TO

296.444
G21   Gaster, Moses.
            The Ketubah.

Temple Israel Library
Minneapolis, Minn.

Please sign your full name on the above card.

Return books promptly to the Library or Temple Office.

Fines will be charged for overdue books or for damage or loss of same.

DEMCO

THE KETUBAH

by
Moses Gaster

Second, augmented edition
Edited with New Introduction and Notes
by
Samuel Gross

HERMON PRESS
NEW YORK

THE KETUBAH

First edition: Rimon Publishing Co Berlin-London, 1923
Second, augmented edition
© Copyright Sepher-Hermon Press Inc.
New York, 1974
LCC Card No. 68-9532
ISBN 0-87203-029-6

Introduction to the New Edition

Fifty years ago, when Dr. Moses Gaster (1856-1939), the learned Haham of the Sephardi community of London, first published this charming monograph on the Ketubah, it reflected more the breadth of his own wide-ranging scholarship than the interests of the contemporary Jewish intellectual community.

In the Ketubah, Gaster claimed to have discovered the richest mine for the study of Jewish culture in all its aspects. To him, the Ketubah was, first and foremost, an as yet untapped source for the study of Jewish history, folklore, anthropology and sociology, as well as a host of lesser disciplines.

Only towards the end of his essay, in what appears to be almost as an afterthought, does Dr. Gaster dwell at some length on the importance of the illuminated ketubah as a genuine Jewish art form concluding with a call for "the immediate collection, examination and preservation of all available Ketubot..."

Predictably, the learned author's enthusiasm for the Ketubah as a cornucopia of Judaic scholarship was received by his contemporaries in the academic community with polite reservation. One reviewer (Louis M. Epstein in *Jewish Quarterly Review*, vol. XV, finds the monograph a "delightful tale" in which are woven together "research, analysis, guide to students and cultural message into one artistic complex." Yet, the same reviewer refuses to share Gaster's enthusiasm for the Ketubah as a vademecum for Judaic research finding such claims overstated. Indeed, in the subsequent half century, Jewish historians and social scientists have made little if any use of ketubot as a tool in their investigations.

Paradoxically, Gaster's cautious endorsement of the illuminated Ketubah as a "genuine" Jewish art object was what generated an avid interest in it as evidenced by the ensuing growth of literature and, in recent years, by the increasing number of collectors of Ketubot, both private and institutional, in search of surviving specimens.

The current keen interest in the subject is best reflected in the recent publication of *The Ketubah* by David Davidovitch, with Foreword by Cecil Roth (E. Lewin-Epstein Ltd., Tel-Aviv, 1969), the first published collection of illuminated ketubot. Important shorter studies have also been written by, among others, Cecil Roth, Ernest Namenyi and Franz Landsberger.

*　*　*　*　*

In the present edition, the eight illustrations of this minor classic have been augmented by nine additional plates. Of these, eight are reproductions of rare ketubot in private and institutional collections never before published, selected for some noteworthy feature or peculiarity as pointed out in the accompanying descriptions.

The ninth specimen is the reproduction of a contemporary American ketubah, a visual testimony both to the vitality of the age-old art of Ketubah illustration and the artistic coming of age of American Jewry.

SAMUEL GROSS

The Ketubot reproduced in this new edition are from the following collections:

The New York Public Library (Plates XIII, XIV, XV)

The Library of the Jewish Theological Seminary of America (Plates IX, X, XI)

Mr. Bernard Zucker, New York (Plates XII, XVI)

Rembrandt Associates, New York (Plate XVII)

For their kind permission, our thanks.

The Publishers

BIBLIOGRAPHY

Davidovitch, David, *The Ketubah: Jewish Marriage contracts through the Ages.* Tel-Aviv, 1968.

Encyclopedia Judaica (German). Berlin, 1928-1934.

Encyclopedia Judaica (English) Jerusalem, 1972

Gutmann, Joseph, *Jewish Ceremonial Art.* New York and London, 1964

The Jewish Encyclopedia, New York, 1901-1906

Landsberger, Franz, "Illuminated Marriage Contracts," *HUCA XXVI, 1955*

Leveen, Jacob, *The Hebrew Bible in Art.* London, 1944.

Morais, Sabato, *Italian Hebrew Literature.* (reprint) New York, 1970.

Mortara, M. *Indice...dei...Rabbini...in Italia.* Padua, 1886.

Narkiss, Bezalel, *Hebrew Illuminated Manuscripts.* Jerusalem, 1969.

Neppi, H. and Gherondi, M.S., *Toledot Gedolei Yisrael.* Trieste, 1853

The New Standard Jewish Encyclopedia. Garden City, 1970

Roth, Cecil, *Gleanings.* New York, 1967

——"The Ketubah in Jewish Art," *Hadassah Magazine.* June, 1969

Shahar, Yeshayahu, *The Feuchtwanger Collection of Jewish Tradition and Art* (Hebrew). Jerusalem, 1971

Synagoga, 2nd ed. Recklinghausen, 1961

LIST OF ILLUSTRATIONS

Bridal Pair .... Page 9

Wedding Ceremony .... Page 54

Ketubah of Ancona .... Plate I

Fragment of a Ketubah from Fostat .... Plate II

Fragment of a Ketubah from Fostat .... Plate III

Ketubah of Gibraltar .... Plate IV

Nuptial Pair .... Plate V

Ketubah of Rome .... Plate VI

Ketubah of Krems .... Plate VII

Detail from a Ketubah of Rivarolo .... Plate VIII

Ketubah of Ferrara, 1627 .... Plate IX

Ketubah of Mantua, 1636 .... Plate X

Ketubah of Verona, 1695 .... Plate XI

Ketubah of Ferrara, 1719 .... Plate XII

Ketubah of Reggio, 1774 .... Plate XIII

Ketubah of Reggio, 1795 .... Plate XIV

Ketubah of Bosetto, 1801 .... Plate XV

Ketubah of Pitiliano, 1843 .... Plate XVI

Ketubah of Belle Harbor, 1974 .... Plate XVII

BRIDAL PAIR.
From an illuminated Prayer-book of the XIVth Century.
Leipzig University Library.

The beginnings of all legal, civil or religious institutions
are lost in the obscurity of the ages. The modern science
of comparative studies rests on this assumption of extreme
antiquity and on the belief that many of them were once
the common property of man, and have slowly developed
under the political and economic changes through which
every nation has passed. The very history of civilization
is the result of these comparative investigations; it shows

9

the way in which our modern civilization has been slowly developed from primitive origins.

One is no longer satisfied with merely chronicling facts or starting the history of nations with some of the written data which have come down to us, however old they may be; for they, already, are the result of previous development and point back to other times when these things had not yet been. The study of man, therefore, from its very earliest beginnings, stands in the forefront of modern investigation and research. I purposely say man in all his manifestations, for we are no longer content to study one thing alone, say ceremony or social life, religious practice or beliefs, or even poetry and legend; all these form a unity. They are closely interwoven, and they depend upon one another and explain one another. One has often to reconstruct the whole system out of small fragments picked up from various parts, and pieced together by the light of similar appearances or systems elsewhere.

The study of folk-lore and anthropology has now assumed a very great importance. It is no longer regarded as dealing with mere tales and legends or describing peculiar practices and ceremonies limited often to one country or to one nation: one has discerned in these very tales or practices survivals of more ancient traditions which go back to prehistoric times. Grimm, the founder of modern folk-lore, already recognized traces of ancient myths in these simple tales, but he only wanted to reconstruct a German mythology out of them. We have since gone much farther afield. We know that many of these figures in which he saw the disguised form of ancient Teutonic gods, recur also in tales of many lands and many peoples far distant from Europe. And so the circle has widened and with it, the comparative study of folk-tales and sagas. And if we find similar tales in ancient oriental literature, of course they destroy the claim based on them formulated for German mythology only, but their importance grows for the much wider outlook of primitive faiths and legends.

The same holds good also for what is called superstition and above all for social and religious ceremonies and practices. A very broad basis has, therefore, been sought for them, and ·the influence which each of these has exercised upon the various nations has been very patiently investigated. Thus we are slowly led back step by step to earliest times and modern students have, therefore, gone to the most primitive races of mankind in order to study their institutions, practices and ceremonies, their beliefs and customs, in order to obtain comprehensive and reliable material for the elucidation of many of the problems of modern life.

Among these problems the greatest has been the relation of the sexes, the position of the women in society and above all, the marriage problem. Under what form does the marriage take place, what gives it validity and in how far is the woman protected? Then come questions of endogamy and exogamy, that is marrying within or outside the clan, people marrying only those of their own family or again on the contrary, where such marriage would not be tolerated by the community. Furthermore, there is the problem of monogamy and polygamy, the difference between the wife and the concubine, the status of the children of such marriages and a large number of other legal and social questions, not to speak of the many ceremonies which accompanied the marriage feast. The marriage by violent abduction, the marriage by purchase and the marriage by consent represent so many stages in the history of man, which must be traced through manifold evolutions in the course of the social development of the community, forming as it were so many steps in the history of civilization. A huge literature has grown up round the subject, showing the importance it has assumed in the modern studies of anthropology and folk-lore. Much unexpected light is thereby shed upon many hitherto insufficiently understood incidents in the ancient history of the world. But it is not here the place to discuss these problems, since I am dealing only with one of the latest phases in that development.

Though from time to time primitive forms can be traced in allusions and incidents in the Biblical narrative, yet it stands already on so high a level of moral and social development that the original stages have long ago been left behind. The community has emerged from those early beginnings and has reached a lofty conception of the relations between man and woman. The purity of life is so often and so intensely insisted upon in the Biblical narrative, that it suffices merely to refer to it to be fully satisfied that in the Biblical period marriage by abduction or marriage by purchase were no longer tolerated. Very heavy penalties were provided for the transgressor and examples are not wanting that such penalties were exacted. In spite of what has often been repeated from interested sides, the position of the women in the Biblical period not only compares favourably with that assigned to the women even in the highest civilised empires of the time, Egypt and Babylon, but far surpasses that which the women occupied centuries later in Greece and Rome.

Comparative study, which is now placed in the forefront in the system of investigation, has also thrown a strong light on the position of women in these countries. And one can go even one step farther and say, that the safe-guards which have been imposed by Biblical and post Biblical Judaism for the protection of their women and for the happiness of married life, have not been reached even in modern times by our boasted civilization. This subject, however, cannot be pursued here much further, for it may lead us into the study of the darker sides of modern life.

One of the means used for the purpose of protecting our Jewish women was the Ketubah or the marriage contract. Originally, the marriage was considered as a purely civil institution, not dependent upon any religious ceremony. It must not be forgotten, however, that a solemn assertion was considered as binding as an oath, and therefore no further ceremony was required which should obtain a specific religious character. Jewish life is so thoroughly permeated with religious consciousness,—every act which a Jew performs is intended to conform to a written or suggested divine ordinance and therefore on every act a Jew is expected to express a blessing,—that it is obvious that such a blessing should also be recited on the occasion of a marriage. And thus a religious feature was introduced to give greater solemnity to the civil act of marriage and to bring it into line with all the other actions under the law. The real object, however, of the Ketubah was to provide as strong a protection of the woman who was about to be married as the civil law could secure. In the first place, the young woman had to be assured that her future husband would not be free to treat her as a mere handmaid or a purchased slave whom he could dismiss at his free will and leave her, without means of subsistence and without help, on the charity of the world. If she brought money from her father's house, or other objects into the newly established household, these had to be safeguarded against possible failure of the husband in his worldly transactions who might otherwise waste her sub-

13

stance; or against the possibility that her husband should be able to take all her property and use it as he chose and then turn her away, poor and broken. The contract, made to meet these contingencies, puts therefore the liabilities upon the man, while it must be pointed out, that no liability except the moral one rests with the woman. The Ketubah is a solemn pledge coupled with an oath, which the man is expected to take before the congregation or before qualified men, that he will perform all the duties and obligations which he voluntarily takes upon himself for the protection of his wife, now in his lifetime and after his death, all of which are entered in that document. If he divorce her, her property goes back to her and if he leave her a widow, part of her property returns to her: in any case, she has something to fall back upon in every circumstance of trouble and distress arising out of her married life.

In order to exemplify the far-reaching importance of the Ketubah from this point of view and from all the others which are going to be discussed in the following pages, I will give presently the translation of at least one or two of these Ketubot or written documents, especially as I am not discussing here the Ketubah from the legal point of view but from the archæological and historical.

One question, however, remains still to be answered. How old is the Ketubah? Since when has this institution been introduced into Jewish life? In the pages of the Bible we find so far no trace of any such written document preceding the marriage or connected with it. In olden times the people did not resort to much correspondence of a private character, not at any rate among the Jews, and notably not before the period of the exile to Babylon. Still, one may infer from another practice that the idea of a written document connected with marriage would not strike the people as a strange institution or a peculiar innovation. For we find that when the severance of the matrimonial tie was contemplated, if a man for one reason or another wished to send his wife away from him, he had to give her a written document, a "letter of severance", of cutting the connection, as it were, called Sepher Keritut, and this only with her consent. This the man had to give into the hands of the woman, in order that she should be able to show to the world that she was no longer married and that if and when she married another man, she did not thereby act contrary to the accepted principle of purity and did not lay herself open to any punishment or transgression. Thus a written document had to be prepared and this principle persists to this very day when the word "Get" has been substituted for the words "Sepher Keritut". Of course, in the case of a woman marrying, there was no necessity to write a document to prove to the world that the couple lived in lawful wedlock. There was no necessity for the woman to prove to anyone else her position and her character as a good Jewish wife: her station in the house was sufficient evidence. But times changed, and just as a woman had to obtain a written document to protect her from slander and her children from worse consequences should she marry another man whilst her former husband was still alive,—she might otherwise have been treated as an adulterous woman,—it became also necessary to protect by a somewhat similar document the position and property of the wife against all possible contingencies. Moreover, the Jews began to travel far and wide and the women left behind had to be provided with some means of protecting the property they held in the name of the husband. The forcible scattering through the exile, furthermore, created new problems with which the leaders of the time had to cope. It is, therefore, very probable that we must trace the beginning of the Ketubah to the period immediately on the return from the exile. Then the Sopher

15

or official scribe, the man who was able not only to copy the Torah but probably also to draw up all the legal contracts, becomes one of the most important personalities in the new Jewish commonwealth.

Again, the stay in the exile in Babylon had taught the Jews among many other things, also the importance of drawing up legal documents. The largest part of the cuneiform inscriptions on the tablets recovered from the ruins of Babylon and Nineveh, consists of contracts, a mass of legal documents relating to every phase of human life. They had been accumulated in those ancient libraries and go a long way to prove how extensive was the practice of drawing up legal documents among the Babylonians. Quickwitted as the Jews were, they did not fail to appreciate the lessons they had learned and to apply them to their own private life.

A problem soon presented itself to those who returned from the exile, which called for the drastic intervention of the scribe Ezra and of Nehemiah. Some of those who had returned, had married women from among the neighbouring nations, but on the insistence of these leaders, the Jews had to divorce them and to take Jewish women. Here then, arose no doubt the necessity of placing upon these men proper obligations for the protection of their newly wedded wives. They should not think they could dismiss them equally quickly, but that they had taken upon themselves serious liabilities and responsibilities.

At the same time, the people were asked to produce proofs of their purity of descent. They had to show their genealogy, Yichus, in order to be able to enjoy all the privileges both as lay man and priest. In order to satisfy a demand which was of such a searching character at the time, it would not have been sufficient for them to trace their line of pedigree as far as their fathers only were concerned. The real problem with which it was intended to grapple was to eliminate the pagan women. The Jews had, therefore, to prove that they were of Jewish descent both on their fathers' and mothers' sides. So, obviously, they must have had some means of satisfying this demand: some written document which would establish beyond doubt their purity of descent, of whichever class they belonged, Israelites, Levites or Cohanim. This is certainly an indication that such documents must have been in existence and that they must have been in general use, if everyone were expected to produce some such documentary evidence for the purpose of proving his father and mother to have been Jews.

Thus the marriage became an institution protected and hedged in by legal documents. Something akin to such legal documents whereby the property of the wife became secured, is found among the remarkable collection of the Jewish - Aramaic Papyri found in Assuan, which are almost contemporary with the period just mentioned. The formula probably was not yet finally fixed: it was more the principle which was recognized and applied. So firmly had this practice been established that in the time of Simeon ben Shetach, in the second century B. C. E., only slight modifications were introduced to make the contract more stringent and to raise, as it were, the dignity of the woman by insisting that a certain amount of dowry should be inserted, to which the woman should always have a right, even if she brought nothing else. The man had always to add in form of gift a certain proportion to the wife's dowry, which thus became her absolute property, under those conditions when she had the right to claim them.

In the book of Tobit which, whatever its age, is certainly anterior to the destruction of the Temple, we find already fully set out the fact of the blessing connected with the marriage ceremony and the writing of a document in presence of the elders of the place. Another proof of the extreme antiquity of the Ketubah, going back to the time before the destruction of the Temple, is the fact discovered by me that the Samaritans, who have the Sepher Keritit, as they call it, the bill of divorce, have also a fully elaborated Ketubah for the marriage, as the marriage contract. A close examination of the documents, made by me, goes a long way to prove that the assumption is correct; namely, that the Ketubah in its actual form, at least as far as the general outline is concerned and the fundamental principle of being a safeguard for the women in Israel in their married life, is of very high antiquity, and one cannot therefore be surprised to find such close similarity between the Samaritan and Jewish documents.

It is not to be assumed that the one borrowed from the other. No hatred is so deep as religious hatred and no fanaticism so ruthless as sectarian fanaticism. Jews have certainly not borrowed from the hated Samaritans or "Kutiim" as they called them in disparagement, nor would the Samaritans, to whom the Judæans were an object of scorn, have borrowed anything from them. The similarity, therefore, must date from a period when this deepseated hatred had not yet developed in so virulent a form and when a practice common to all could easily be appropriated by each of them independently.

The high importance which I claim for the Ketubah will be the result of minute investigations of each one of the peculiar features which distinguish a document, which has played such a decisive rôle in Jewish family life; and I am selecting two typical ones, one Italian, of which a facsimile is given and the other Sephardic belonging to one of the descendants of the exiles from Spain, since it is fully characeristic of these Ketubot with their many remarkable features. The latter agrees in all details

with the one reproduced here*) except for the fuller genea-
logies and the dowry. I have translated the various formulæ,
titles of honour etc. for reasons given hereafter in these
pages, just because of the specific value which I assign
to them.

Specimen 1.**)

KETUBAH OF ANCONA.

On the 4th day of the week, on the 14th day of Nisan, in the year 5536
from the creation of the world according to the era which we are
counting, here in Ancona which is situated on the borders of the sea
and is close to the rivers of Asfa and Pimocena, the young, respected
honoured Rabbi Moses Michael — may the Lord protect him — son
of the respected scholar and perspicacious Rabbi Judah of Ascoli —
may the Lord protect him — said unto the young chosen virgin, the
honoured and modest damsel, Esther — blessed of all women in the
home — daughter of the worthy, highly-placed, his reverence (Haber)
(a man holding the diploma of an associate rabbi) our honoured master
and teacher, Joshua Shabetai of Ascoli — may the Lord protect him:
"Be thou my wife according to the law of Moses and Israel. I, with
the help of heaven, will work for thee, honour, support, maintain and
clothe thee in accordance with the custom of Jewish husbands, who
work for their wives, honour, support, maintain and clothe them in
truth. And I have given 200 Zuzai, the mohar, in lieu of thy virginity
which are due unto thee, and I will give thee thy food, clothing, and thy
wants and will live with thee in conjugal relations according to the
way of the world." And the damsel Esther, the virgin bride, consented
and became the wife of the honourable Rabbi Moses Michael before
mentioned. And this is the dowry which she brought from her father's
house; 600 scudi, each of the value of 10 favole; namely, 200 of such
scudi of recognized value in coin (money), 100 scudi gold and silver
ornaments and beautiful pearls and 300 scudi of the above mentioned,
in clothing of wool, linen and silk, and household goods and bed linen.
And the above mentioned bridegroom, Moses Michael, consented to
add to this amount from his own property and money 120 scudi apart
from the amount mentioned above. Thus the whole amount of this
Ketubah, the dowry and the addition, is 720 scudi, exclusive of the
200 zuzim, which are the very essence of the Ketubah. Then said the
bridegroom, Moses Michael, unto her: "I take upon myself and upon my
heirs after me, the responsibilities of this Ketubah, the dowry and the
additional sums, that they should be paid from the property I possess
now or may possess afterwards wherever it be under the heavens, and
with or without obligations (real or personal). All this shall be pledged and
mortgaged to pay out this Ketubah and the additions thereto, to the
last, even the mantle on my shoulders, during my lifetime or after my

*) Plate IV. **) Plate I.

life, even from this day for evermore." And the above mentioned bridegroom, Moses Michael, has taken upon himself the stringent interpretation of this Ketubah and of the conditions, according to the stringent interpretation of all the Ketubot which are customary to be drawn up in favour of the daughters of Israel, the modest, pure ones, by our Sages of blessed memory. It is not to be treated as an illusory obligation or as a simple formal draft. And we, the undersigned witnesses have obtained from the bridegroom, Moses Michael, son of the respected, exalted, scholar, and man of understanding, Rabbi Judah of Ascoli, in favour of the virgin bride Esther now his wife, the daughter of the respected and exalted Haber Joshua Shabetai of Ascoli, everything that is written and explained heretofore, through the legal formality of Kinyan by means of an instrument legally fit for the purpose, and everything is now valid, agreed and established.

Then follow the signatures of the two witnesses only, that of the bridegroom being missing.

Specimen 2.

KETUBAH OF GIBRALTAR.
Cod. Gaster No. 1653.

In a good sign and with propitious luck, and in the year of good will and prosperity!

On the 4th day of the week, on the 8th day of the month of Heshvan, in the year 5658 from the creation of the world, according to the era which we count, here in the town of Gibraltar, the bridegroom who bears the good, resplendent name, the wise, of holy seed, the honourable Abraham, a pure Sephardi, the son of the honourable, who bears a good name, the exalted gentleman, the uplifted one in name and praise, the wise (Haham) and perspicacious one, of holy seed, the honoured Rabbi and teacher Isaac, a pure Sephardi, the son of the honoured one, bearing a good name, the profoundly versed rabbi, the pious, the meek, of holy seed, our honoured master and teacher Abraham — may his memory be for life in the everlasting world and his merit protect us, Amen! — the author of the book "Berith Aboth", son of the honoured rabbi of good name, the chief rabbi, the cabbalist, the son of holy ones (Martius), our honoured master and rabbi Judah — may his memory be for life in the everlasting world! — the author of the book "Ma'or Vashamesh", son of the righteous and pious one, the wonderful rabbi whose glory is a crown for our heads, the divine cabbalist, our honoured master and teacher Abraham—may his memory be for life in the everlasting world! — the author of the precious and pure book "Zechut Aboth", son of the honoured Rabbi with the good name, the great renowned rabbi, the divine cabbalist, our honoured master and teacher Judah — may his memory be for life everlasting and may his merit protect us, amen! may such be the Divine Will! — son of that righteous, great rabbi, the elder in the judgment seat, our honoured master and rabbi Abraham —

may his memory be for life in the world everlasting and may his merit protect us, amen, may such be the Divine Will! — surnamed K—, said unto the honoured and pleasant choice of the beloved, high in grace, Donna Florence — blessed among the women in the home — the virgin bride, daughter of the honoured and perspicacious one, who bears a good and respected name — may the Lord protect him and keep him alive! — Rabbi Isaac, a pure Sephardi — son of the honoured one who bears a good name, the venerable and prespicacious one, who fears sin more than many of the multitude, the honoured Rabbi David, — whose rest be in the Garden of Eden! — son of one who bears an honoured name, the exalted and pious one, Rabbi Levi, — whose rest be in the Garden of Eden! — surnamed K—: "Be thou my wife, according to the law of Moses and Israel. By the word and help of Heaven I will work and cherish thee, I will maintain and provide for thee, I will support and keep thee according to the practice of Jewish men who work and cherish, maintain and provide for, support and keep their wives in truth. And I give unto thee, the dowry of thy virginity and I will keep and support thee and all thy wants, and live with thee in conjugal relations according to the way of the world." And this bride agreed of her free will and she became his wife. Then the bridegroom of his own free will, agreed to add from his own property to the principal of this Ketubah, an amount to complete the sum of 600 pesas fuertos of good silver Spanish coin of this year, which is current here in the town of Gibraltar — may our town be rebuilt, amen! Of his own free will, this Abraham, the bridegroom provided for her four cubits of ground and a stone. He made her a complete gift, to be included in this Ketubah, of an additional sum of 600 pesas fuertos, of good Spanish coin, of the kind above mentioned. And the dowry which the bride brought from her father's house, and her presents be it in clothes or jewels or furniture, the bridegroom, Abraham, accepted of his own free will, at the value of 600 pesas fuertos, of good Spanish coin, of the kind above mentioned. And the total sum contained in this Ketubah amounts, with the principal and additions of the gifts and dowry, to 1800 pesas fuertos of good silver as above mentioned. And the Rabbi Abraham, the bridegroom, took upon himself that he would not marry another woman in addition, except by her consent and with her good will, and that he would not take her from this country to another country without her consent and of her own free will and that if, God forbid, he marry another woman, without her consent or her good will, then he would have to repay everything to which he had now bound himself, and he would divorce her with a proper "Get" at once. And this contract shall be binding upon him and shall apply to him in accordance with the legal strength of the contract applied to the tribe of Reuben and Gad. And also the bridegroom, Abraham, has taken upon himself all the legal responsibilities arising from this Ketubah in its entirety, the principal, the additions, and the gifts of the dowry, and has taken the responsibilities also for his heirs, by pledging according to the ordinances of the Sages — may their memory be blessed — all his property, movable and immovable, which he possesses and may possess. This is not to be treated as an illusory or a mere formal contract. And we have obtained from the bridegroom, Rabbi Abraham, through the legal

21

formality of Kinyan and by means of money as an instrument legally fit for the purpose, the consent for everything that has been written and clearly set out above. And the bridegroom, Rabbi Abraham, took upon himself a solemn oath by handshake and by mentioning the name of the Holy One, before God, blessed be He! And in conformity with all this he took the oath in His great, mighty, and awe-inspiring Name, in truth and uprightness, without any intent to deceive, to keep and observe and perform all that is written and set out clearly concerning him in the above document. And all this has been done in accordance with the rite and statute the latest and most recent ones, by which we are guided, and which have been agreed upon and adopted among the holy community who have been exiled from Castilia — may the Lord avenge them and be gracious, may He protect them and show pity and be merciful and keep them and help them, He who keeps the truth for ever from now unto everlasting! For all these obligations of the dowry have been accepted by the bridegroom, by this complete and perfect contract, and all is now valid, agreed and established.

It must be remembered that the history of our people is unlike that of any other nation. It embraces all the ages and covers all the continents. The emigration of Jews from Palestine starts from Biblical times and the changes through which our people have passed continue to this very day. They are still going on. No task therefore is so difficult as to compile a history of the Jews. Historical documents of a reliable value are few and scarce. It is almost by indirect inference that we are often able to deduct the settlement of Jews in one place or another. There must have existed innumerable settlements of which hitherto no trace has been found, and many a problem to which allusion will be made hereafter arises from the difficulty of establishing this fact. In the first place there is the problem whether the Jews have lived in a certain country, then the question as to how far back that settlement can be traced and when it has come to an end. When have the Jews disappeared from this or the other locality? I take at once the example of Babylon. Large masses of Jews were living in that country down to late

Mohammedan times. Their number could be counted probably by millions, and yet with the exception of a few towns, most of the latter have disappeared.

It is, however, of the highest importance to be able to determine, exactly if possible, the places where the Jews lived, the local organizations which they established, the position which the men and women enjoyed, their relative wealth or poverty, their educational successes; for much will depend upon a satisfactory answer to these questions. We must remember that those countries in the East were the centres of great political and above all of religious movements. What part did the Jews play in assisting to shape the religion of Zoroaster, the teachings of Mani, the founder of Manichæism, and a large number of other heterodox movements, like Sabæism; not to speak of the form which Christianity assumed under the Gnostic influences and others, nay the whole development of the Syriac literature.

I take this merely as one out of innumerable examples. For in the same manner one could ask questions concerning the old Jewish inhabitants of Arabia and Ethiopia, of Armenia and Southern Russia, of Italy and Spain, of Egypt and the African Continent; and yet it would be very difficult indeed to give any definite reply with the aid of the few references preserved in Jewish literature. And even these are often subject to the personal bias of the author, or to his qualification as a writer, and the accuracy of his statements and observations.

True history, however, can only be built upon a solid basis of incontrovertible facts. These are certificates of birth and death, or tombstones. The latter, however, are not always an unerring guide, owing to the fact that the tombstones are sometimes intended to be monuments to those who erected them rather than to those for whom they have been erected. Exuberant admiration or an enthu-

23

siasm carried too far attempts to appreciate the merit of the departed far beyond his deserts, and may lead those who attempt to decipher the ancient inscriptions to very wrong conclusions. They are also individualistic in as much as with rare exceptions only the name of the deceased and his father are mentioned, and in the case of a woman that of her husband. But used with caution and with a critical mind, these tombstones yield no doubt a very rich harvest to the local historian, and are often very helpful in forging genealogical links between various generations, which prove of great interest and value.

Again it must be mentioned that very few cemeteries have been preserved and not every one interred had the means for such a tombstone.

Nothing on the other hand can compare with the marriage contract, the Ketubah, in fullness of detail from every point of view, and the object of this investigation is to bring out all the facts which can be gleaned from a careful study of the Ketubah.

In the first place its historical accuracy, reliability and universal application can not be doubted. The whole sanctity and morality of the Marriage is intimately bound up with the Ketubah, which is moreover the only security for the wife in case of her husband's death. Everything depended upon the woman having a Ketubah, and upon this Ketubah being drawn up in accordance with all the minute prescriptions of the law

Rich or poor, old or young, whoever was married had to have such a Ketubah. It was not the privilege only of the rich like the ornamental tombstones, but it was an obligatory deed which every one had to provide before marriage.

We can imagine therefore the vast multitude of such documents counting by millions which have been written during the last 2000 years in all the lands where Jews have lived. An immense material, almost incalculable in its riches, is contained in this unlimited number of Ketubot which must have existed. Unfortunately they have also perished to a very large extent, for no importance has been attached to them by the generation which followed almost immediately after those for whose benefit they had been written. With the death of the possessor all value of the Ketubah seems to have vanished, and yet as will be shown the Ketubah is the richest mine of Jewish History in all its aspects.

I take in the first place the historical accuracy. Even on tombstones there are often curiously enough mistakes in dates. The mason who cuts the stone seems to have often been very careless; and after all, a mistake in the date carried no further consequences, except the temporary misleading of those who tried afterwards to decipher the year, and very few have ever troubled to do so. Not so the Ketubah: everything depended on the accurate date when a marriage took place. The dates of the births of the children may have been affected by it, and many a claim of the woman could have been vitiated by a wrong date having been entered in her marriage contract. The first line, therefore, of a Ketubah consists of the accurate date. The era is given, the name of the month, the day of the month and the day of the week. And here already we are confronted by a peculiar problem of Jewish Chronology. The Jews did not have one single era. At least two eras are known to have been used by the Jews to this very day, the Seleucid, an era known as the era of the Shetarot the starting point being about 311 before the common era which is used to this very day among the Jews of Arabia and Persia and the other, the era of Creation, used mostly in Europe. There were besides, other eras like that of the Destruction of the Temple which is still referred to in the Sephardic Service of the Fast Day of the 9th of Ab. During the Evening service the Hazan mentions that era to the assembled congregation.

It has not yet been definitely established when and where one era succeeded in supplanting the other, but by means of these Ketubot, if preserved, we would be able to establish almost to a day the place where one era succeeded the other.

Immediately after the date the locality is mentioned where the marriage is taking place, and as there were often towns of a similar name in distant parts of the world, and sometimes even in the same country, care is taken to differentiate most minutely between them. The rivers that flow through the town are mentioned, and if the town is situated at the border of the sea, this fact is carefully noted.

I am not touching now upon the importance which this information has for Geography, for if we had a large number of old Ketubot, many a doubtful point in mediæval and ancient Geography could easily be settled. Old places have disappeared, others have arisen, and the old names have often been forgotten or so mutilated in later times as not easily to be recognized.

Take Palestine. Many a town mentioned in the Bible and even in the Talmud can no longer be identified, and even the old Onomastica of Eusebius and Jerome are insufficient help to solve the problem where Capernaum on the Lake of Genezareth, was situated. But the mention of the name of the town is of still higher value to the Jewish historian, for he could learn from the Ketubah, by the mere mention of the place, that Jews lived as a community in that and that place in such and such a year. New names would thus be added to the map of the Jewish Diaspora. Many an empty space on that map could easily be filled, and we would obtain a more ample survey of the Jewish settlements throughout the length and breadth of all the continents.

How precious would it not be for us to find a Ketubah of the first Jewish settlers in America, the date on which a marriage had been celebrated between a Jew and a Jewess in a certain part of Mexico, or Peru, or in the higher latitudes. It would be of the utmost importance, for this would be a fact which no sophistry, however ingenious, could dispute. All the old settlements of Spanish Jews have practically disappeared, their archives dispersed if they ever had any, and as for the Ketubot, I doubt if any of them are still in existence. Yet in view of this study on the importance of the Ketubah, the one or the other may be stimulated to co-operate in a search for these lost and hitherto ignored but nevertheless valuable documents. How important would it be for us if we could discover some Ketubot of the ancient settlers in Armenia, or in the south of Russia, where later on arose the kingdom of the Chazars, who afterwards became Jews: or of their descendants who travelled with the Hungarians into Panonia (modern Hungary) and lived there as independent knights in their castles, until they were slowly absorbed. This would explain, to a large extent, the judaising movement in Transylvania which culminated in the Sabbatarian movement in the seventeenth century. Similarly, no one could underestimate the importance of the Jewish settlers in the Balkan Peninsula from ancient times if proved by the existence of such Ketubot. For again, that might explain many religious and sectarian movements afterwards called "heretic" in the Byzantine Empire and, above all, among the Slavonic nations along the Danube. And so one might carry on similar investigations in the south of France and elsewhere wherever spiritual forces were at work, which were repressed and exterminated by the violence of the Church. One single

Ketubah from each of these places would outweigh a mass of hypothetical historiography, for no one could gainsay the fact here irrefutably proved by such a document. For wherever a Ketubah has been written, one is justified in assuming the existence of a community in that place, with a man versed in the Law and capable of writing in accordance with the old prescriptions, witnesses capable of signing, and men able to perform the religious ceremonies.

And to come to modern times, what could give us a clearer insight into the settlement of the Jews in Poland and in the ancient Pale, than a systematic collection of such Ketubot and a careful examination of all the geographical data which they contain? But we are only on the fringe of the subject.

Immediately after the date and the place, the names of the bride and bridegroom and those of their parents are mentioned. Here again we must go step by step and try to exhaust all the information that can be gathered trom these data.

There are first the very names. Any one who has studied the Onomatology of our people will find that it offers a vast field for philological and even psychological investigation. Zunz has already collected a large number of names borne by Jews and Jewesses, but a real study of the names and surnames has not yet been undertaken. This must be carried out according to periods, and according to countries. We would then be struck by the fact that the Jews assumed names current among the other nations in whose midst they lived, only when social conditions brought them close to one another. When there is an intimate intercourse between Jew and non-Jew, the Jew will as often as not approximate his name to that of the Gentile. En Bonet in Narbon, Abduraham in Spain, Anatoli in Italy, Capsali in Byzance and so on, prove this case. One could go very far back in the study of Jewish names borrowed from the Gentiles and adapted as their own. The very Maccabæan kings had two names, one Greek and one Hebrew which can be read on the coins struck by them; and again in the catacombs one can find Greek and Latin names used by Jews. Not a few of the sages bore strange names. But there are also changes in names which are of a psychological interest; e. g., no Talmudic scholar will assume a Biblical name or with rare exceptions. None will call himself Moses. During the period of the second Temple, Greek names came in vogue, but also the Hebrew names bear a peculiar character of their own. This disappears in later times when a large number of surnames suddenly appeared. To trace these philologically would be a very interesting subject indeed, and to compare them with contemporary surnames among non-Jews would cast an important light upon the relation in which the Jews stood to their neighbours. No Jew in Russia, Rumania or Poland ever dreamt, say fifty years ago, of calling himself by a Slavonic name, like Nicolai, Stan, Ivan, Wladimir, Youri etc.

Still more interesting are the names of the women. The lists drawn up by rabbinical authors anxious to provide an exact formula for the orthography of such names in marriage contracts and above all in Bills of Divorce (Get), are far from even remotely exhausting the immense number of names found in these Ketubot.

There are then sometimes six or seven names on a Ketubah as exemplified in the Spanish Ketubah given above; the bride and bridegroom, the fathers of both, and one, two or even more witnesses at the bottom of the document. Now these names are often accompanied by titles, occasionally even by a string of titles. These denote the social standing in the Community, like Parnas, Haber, Yakar, Nichbad, Naalah, Maskil, Nabon, Haham, Rabbi,

Morenu etc. Each of these titles has a meaning of its own. In the first place they prove that for a man to bear such a title he must form part of a settled communal organisation, and by the string of titles added to the name, we realise that there must have been degrees in the honours assigned to the bearers of such titles, which again points to a large community where people were very anxious to have their status clearly defined and properly set out.

The Jewish communities, however, were not organized everywhere on the same basis, and the titles which the leaders of the community hold vary from time to time and from country to country. One has only to see the string of titles on the Ketubah of the Prince of the Exile, Resch Galuta, which has also been preserved in letters or petitions addressed to him, and in the Hashkabot by Rabbinites and Karaites. Of these titles I am preparing a special study for which I have collected large material. It is sufficient for my purpose here, however, to indicate the vast possibilities contained in these titles of honour, found in the Ketubot.

By their similarity or dissimilarity one would be able to establish the relation in which one community stood in its organization to another community. Thus one could slowly work back in each case to a more ancient one which had been the model for the others. Whether Babylonian or Palestinian influences had been at work could then be easily determined by such a comparison. And the relation between the holders of these various titles would become much clearer than we are able as yet to see, owing to the indifference with which these titles have been treated at a later period.

There is still something more to be learned from these names. It is often impossible for a Jew to trace his genealogy many generations back. Herein we see again the tragedy of our people. The members of one family may be carried far and wide like the scattered leaves of a tree shaken by the storm, and dropped in various places. After one or two generations the connection with the past is forgotten, the links are irremediably broken. People who have to face the trials of life at every turn cannot foster or develop pride of ancestry. They have no mind for antiquarian research which often yields only fictitious pedigrees for those who in affluence would like to add the pride of descent to the pride of money. The only means by which one could trace such pedigrees are the Ketubot and notably such Ketubot like the Spanish one printed here. The Sephardic Jews were not satisfied with merely mentioning the names of the fathers of the bride and bridegroom, but carried their pedigrees as far back as they were able to trace, sometimes five or six generations or even more. No doubt they must have had their own chain of pedigree (Shalsheleth Ha Yuhasin) and it becomes evident that by means of such chains they were able to perpetuate that pedigree in a tangible manner in the Ketubah and to hand it on from generation to generation. This would explain e. g. why the Abarbanels believed themselves to be descendants of the house of David. Probably they were able to trace their genealogy from such undoubted evidence as the Ketubah offers, to a Babylonian or Palestinian descendant of the House of David. The writers of such Ketubot were, however, not satisfied merely with mentioning the names of these numerous links in the genealogical chain, but when these men happened to be scholars and above all authors of books, the scribes did not fail to add to the names the titles befitting their position in the world of learning, and at the same time to mention the books which they had written. This was much more than a mere gallery of ancestors, empty faces painted on canvas, sometimes of

of similar documents. A vast number can be adduced to prove this fact, that among the Jews a long line of scholars follow one upon another, father, son and grandson and so on in an unbroken line: they are all spiritual leaders, Rabbis, etc. who carry on the tradition, the son sometimes reaching the excellence of his father, sometimes even surpassing it, his son perhaps not reaching the same high level, but still rising high above his contemporaries. And so we have the constant flow and ebb but without a shallow. And in the Ketubah we have the undoubted proof of these facts. If we could only collect all those belonging to one family what wonderful pedigrees could we not trace, and what remarkable facts as to the inner life of these scholars could not be evolved out of the study of these documents.

In the course of time Gentiles also embraced the Jewish faith, for in the early centuries Judaism proved to be a faith which appealed to the masses, and at one time in the history of modern civilization, there was a period when Judaism might have become the world religion. It was at that critical moment that Christianity stepped in, and by demanding practically no sacrifice, neither Sabbath nor Observance, nor Circumcision, nor abstinence from certain foods, etc. and for other reasons which need not be discussed here, was able to wean the masses from their Judaizing tendency. Still there was always a number of proselytes, though it would be very difficult to trace them in the absence of documentary evidence. A few of the more prominent have not been forgotten but no record has been kept of the lowly and the humble; these established their record only in the Ketubah. There they are either entered as *Gere Tsedek*, righteous proselytes who had embraced the Jewish faith from a feeling of pure love, or they are called sons or daughters of our forefather Abraham. This designation would give us a clue to their origin, and if we had a large collection of old Ketubot it would be possible to reconstruct the history of the Jewish Mission. It would then be possible to establish the time and the countries where such missionary activity was conducted, how long it was allowed, and what attitude the Jews themselves took up towards these new members of the faith. To which rank in society did they belong, with whom did they intermarry, with the rich or with the poor? And in this wise also the question of the purity or the mixed character of the race in modern times could be better established than by the wild hypotheses of the mixture of the Jewish Race, advanced by the members of a school of investigation which aims ostensibly at obtaining purely scientific results, but which cannot free itself from hostile bias, nay uses this very science as a cloak. There are again scholars who are interested in tracing Jewish blood in the veins of the Gentiles, often the result of apostasy or of vaingloriousness. But it is more interesting to discover if possible, whether indeed non-Jewish blood may have been mixed with ours and to what extent, for if so, it would be homage paid to us and to our faith, since it always meant a heavy sacrifice on the part of those who joined their lives with ours, and dared the consequences.

All these considerations, however, are overshadowed, and to my mind to an extraordinary degree, by a fact disclosed through the Ketubah to which, so far as I am aware, no attention has yet been paid. The fact to which I am referring is that by the means of these Ketubot alone we may be able to trace the names and the families also of the mothers of our great men who have played such important rôles in the history of our people.

No one can deny that the mother has not only an equal share in the mental and physical qualities of the child, but that very often the impression which she leaves upon it is far greater than that made by the father. If we knew e. g. who was the mother of Maimonides and could trace her pedigree, a key might be found to the mind of one of the greatest men produced by our people. We should like to know also who was the mother of Rashi, that loving, modest, great interpreter of Bible and Talmud, then that of Nachmanides, the profound exponent of mysticism or of Jehudah Halevi, the Master Poet, or again of Aben Ezra, the keen mathematician, critical exeget and at the same time a real wandering Jew. The mother of Sabbatai Zebi might be an object of interest, as well as that of Joseph Karo, who with his systematic legal mind "decked the table" for the Jewish masses, or again that of Spinoza who has exercised such a profound influence upon modern philosophy. None of these can be found except by rare chance through the discovery of an unknown tombstone or stray illusion.

But should such information come to light it would then be seen that Jewish women played an important rôle in Jewish life. Their education could not have been neglected. They must have had well stocked minds if their offspring showed such eminence, which always rests upon the rich spiritual inheritance that comes from both their parents and grandparents. I consider this as one of the most important results of a thorough investigation of all existing Ketubot, which ought to be collected before they are entirely lost.

The Ketubah, however, contains some more details also of entrancing interest. We must steadily keep in mind that it is a contract between a bridegroom and his bride. The bridegroom, therefore, makes a gift as an earnest of his desire of marrying the damsel in question, of a certain sum fixed by our sages at a nominal figure. There is no woman who is not worth such an attention. It is not a price which he pays: Jewish women are not offered for sale, but it is the form by which he binds himself, to deposit a certain sum in favour of the wife, if and when she should ever have recourse to it. There is a difference in the naming of the coin which is taken as a standard. In some documents it is called Tsori (Tyrian), unless the original meaning has been forgotten, and should be read "Tsoref" purified silver,—while in others the name Zuzim or something else appears. These are all indications of economic changes which have supervened in the course of time, and have contributed to establish separate Minhagim, according to the use of the word employed in the document; often the explanatory words are added, "according to such and such a Minhag". A comparative study of these Minhagim may help us to trace the connection between one community and the other, and the historical reasons which have often contributed towards shaping the form of this kind of Ketubah. But of this a little more later on.

I will dwell now on the economic aspect revealed by the Ketubah. This fixed sum is an indispensable portion of the settlement made by the husband. But the woman has also a dowry and the bridegroom increases the amount which the woman brings by another gift of his own, and thus creates a real settlement for the protection of his wife in case of death or economic troubles. If there be a chapter in Jewish history which has scarcely been touched upon except for some work undertaken quite recently by modern writers, it is that of the economic position of the Jews through the Ages. We would like to know the life of a rich Jew, what amount constituted riches, what form luxury took and whether he indulged in it; what again were the household goods, the furniture, the character and costliness of the robes of the women, the value of the jewellery and other details, which no painter has yet delineated, and of which hitherto scarcely anything has been known. Of course, one can imagine, that the Jews and Jewesses would also conform in their outward dress and in their home life to the example set by the nation in whose midst they lived. But this depended upon the political status in which they found themselves. When treated as equals and holding public offices, they would certainly conform to the general way of the world, but when, as in Byzance and later on in the narrow streets of the Ghetto, they were driven in upon themselves, the question is naturally whether they indulged in these luxuries in the home, in beautiful robes or jewellery, which they dared not display to the world outside. And if one remembers the costumes prescribed to the Jews with the yellow badges and peculiar hats, one is justified in asking whether these prescriptions were applied also to the women and if so, how they arranged their costumes accordingly. It is unnecessary to point out the immense value of the contribution which a knowledge of these details would make to the history of costume, but it is only through the Ketubah that we gain a true insight into all these details. They are, moreover true to nature, absolutely true and reliable, for no man would have accepted a fictitious dowry, and undertaken the full responsibility for a list of clothes, jewellery, house furniture, etc. which only existed in the imagination. In these Ketubot then, at any rate in a vast number of them, a detailed list was given of every object of any value which the bride brought as a dowry into the house of her future husband, given to her by her parents in addition to a certain amount of money. A minute valuation was made of each of the objects enumerated, and the sum total very carefully inserted. To this, the bridegroom added an equivalent sum, or such a sum as was agreed upon by the contracting parties. In the two Ketubot given above, we find some specimens of such a dowry given in detail. There are others, especially oriental ones, which contain a still more minute and elaborate description of the various objects brought by the bride as a dowry from her parents. The names of the silks and embroidered brocades also show what kind of trade must have flourished at that time in the town where the marriage took place, and the way in which the Jews knew how to use all these beautiful things for their own luxurious home life. Silk pillows, costly dresses, many other beautiful things are in a way a revelation and a valuable contribution to the history of trade. A collection of such Ketubot with long lists of dowries would help us to appreciate better the conditions under which the rich and, proportionately, the poor people lived in different times and in various countries. One cannot exaggerate from every point of view the importance of these objects mentioned in the lists of dowries. Incidentally, some information can be gathered towards the study of the exchange value of the coinage, for in each country the common currency is mentioned in appraising the value of the objects forming the dowry. This in itself is of no small interest to the study of commerce and the value of things in olden times; for each of the articles mentioned is sometimes valued separately.

But the contracting parties were not satisfied with mentioning only the coinage of the place in which they lived: for as is well known many states or provinces had mints of their own, and even to day it is no easy task to discover a common standard for all the coins that were issued from these numerous mints. It so happened that sometimes the contracting parties came from different states; in consequence, it became necessary to give in the Ketubah the equivalent value of the money mentioned in the coinage of another state. Sometimes the Venetian Scudi are taken as the standard, but at other times, in Spanish Ketubot, especially in those of the emigrants to other parts of the world, the Doros are mentioned and are taken as the standard. In the east, oriental money is mentioned, and in the Samaritan Ketubot other coins are mentioned which have since gone out of use. The tendency to retain the old form with great rigidity shows itself again in matters concerning the standard coin. It partook of that legal accuracy so essential to the validity of the Ketubah, and the people were loth to alter it; hence the archaic character of the coins mentioned in these documents. The best proof can be seen in the retention of the primitive formula which assigns to the virgin bride a gift of 200 "Zuzim" either of the Tyrian standard or that of pure silver. The exact exchange value of that amount is an archæological problem, or rather a numismatic one, and here again the science of Numismatics would gain considerably if a large number of such Ketubot could be examined from the point of view of the coins mentioned and the exchange value found in these Ketubot.

Take a case from Poland of the fifteenth or sixteenth century. Studied from this aspect what a flood of light would be thrown on the economic condition of the Jews in that part of the world just at a period when other documents are scarce. To reconstruct that economic condition is now a matter of mere guesswork, and any attempt to realise the life of the Jews during this period would be almost impossible. How great would be the contrast with the economic conditions of the Jews in the same country after the Khmelnitski pogroms or after the Frankist aberration in the eighteenth century which brought untold misery on the Jews of Poland. Or again, going up the stream of history, how important would it be to be able to compare a Ketubah written before the Crusades had swept over the Rhine Province and Central Europe with one written a century later. How would Scott have been able to describe the expected dowry of Rebecca in his "Ivanhoe"! A few glimpses of course have been vouchsafed by the Ketubot found in the Genizah, which carry the story back almost to the ninth century; and if we allow our imagination to roam still farther back, there is among the documents of Assuan, the Papyri of the 4th and 5th centuries before the common era, a record of the dowry of Mibtahya. Each line of these documents is pregnant with inexhaustible information, as is shown by the literature which has grown up round them since their discovery some twenty years ago.

The pledges which the bridegroom takes upon himself are not, however, limited to finance alone, but in many of the Ketubot we find other obligations into which he enters. There is an historic background and justification for such obligations and if studied in that light, they offer us another means of obtaining a deeper insight into the tragedy of our people. There are documents in which the husband pledges himself not to travel without the consent of his wife. He is not to take adventurous voyages or to expose himself to the risks of travellers and traders in times when the roads were infested by knights or common highwaymen, aristocratic robbers or simple bandits; for no journey was more fraught with danger than that of a Jew travelling in far away lands, and carrying costly merchandise with him.

Years might pass before the news could reach a disconsolate woman who had become a widow long before. And again years might pass without any news reaching her at all. She would not know whether she was still the wife of a living husband or a widow. She would be what is called in legal terminology an Agunah, unable to remarry, powerless to claim her property under the marriage contract, full of responsibilities and without any possible legal relief. Such clauses pointed to times of danger and also to a practice which must have been very common when Jews were forced to travel far and wide. It was a time when every ship might easily have been captured by pirates and the whole company sold into slavery, while there was scarcely any ship that left any Mediterranean port in which Jews did not sail; and the poor woman would then be asked to part with her last farthing in order to ransom her husband from the bondage of captivity and slavery.

How great this danger was is made manifest by the innumerable societies established by the Jews for Pidyon Shebuyim, for the "ransom of captives". Many an old fragment found in the Genizah tells us of the self-sacrificing activity of the ancient communities in such work of liberation. Even the Sephardic Congregration of Bevis Marks had for close upon two centuries such a fund called Resgato do Cautivos, and large sums were often going through Venice to other places for the ransom of captives. This state of things is reflected in that apparently innocent clause in the Ketubah by which the husband should not venture upon a journey without the consent of his wife.

Another clause inserted in it is to the effect that the husband is to provide for the proper burial of his wife should she predecease him. This is often found in Spanish documents. What a tragedy lies behind this grim clause. It brings before our eyes the picture of the wholesale emigration of hundreds of thousands of fugitives from Spain, fleeing from the sword and from the pyre, not knowing whither to go, nor where to find a resting place, sleeping the night in one place, and leaving the next morning; driven from country to country and carrying their women and children with them.

One can understand then the insertion of such a clause, the imposition of such a condition upon a man who, in the midst of that tremendous upheaval, intended to marry. One of the first conditions to be demanded would be a settled life. The man must know where he would be living, whether his life would be safe and whether he would be able to provide for his family; to a certain extent it also implies that they would live within a Jewish Community, which had a cemetery of its own, and with it the possibility of a Jewish burial, or at any rate close enough to such a settlement to be able to carry out the last duties. One can easily imagine the horror with which the men and women of the time contemplated the thought that should death supervene, even the last peaceful repose among their own would be denied to them, and that their bodies might perhaps be thrown into a ditch or into a common grave with the gentile paupers, forlorn and forgotten, with no trace left of their existence, and no sign to mark their last resting place. This part of the Ketubah has often been written in tears of blood instead of ink.

And then coming towards the end of the document we find that it is signed by witnesses, in order to give to the Ketubah the validity of a contract legally drawn up. A new set of names is thus added to those mentioned in the body of the document. They had to be men of substance and character, otherwise their signatures would have been of no value, and sometimes they added a short indication as to their position, like Parnas, Hazan, etc. Occasionally in an old document but more frequently in more recent Ketubot, the bridegroom also signs the Ketubah and thus in addition we have another autograph. This is a very

43

rare occurrence in our literature, for most of the ancient MSS. have come down to us in copies made by Scribes, sometimes long after the death of the author: with the exception of a few autograph letters and a few MSS. signed by Maimonides, scarcely any other genuine signature has come down to us from the great men of the past. How interesting, for example, it would be to have the autograph signature of one of the Princes of the Exile, the heads of the great colleges, scholars, financiers or politicians; one could perhaps glean from the signature something of the character of the men, for nothing is so characteristic as the writing of a signature, and a whole science exists which professes to decipher the inner life of a man from a few letters written by him. Although the signature of the bridegroom on the Ketubah does not seem to be a very ancient general practice, that of the witnesses was indispensable and goes back to ancient times, for without it the document would be invalid. And if we compare the Samaritan Ketubot referred to before with the documents found among the Papyri of Assuan, one cannot but be struck by almost the identical form in which these witnesses sign. This comparison is again of great importance, for on the one hand it establishes the high antiquity of the formula and manner of drawing up such a document, and on the other it shows the changes and transformations which have taken place and assists us in determining the times and conditions under which these changes have come about.

It shows how small and insignificant the changes have been when compared with the rigidity with which the general form of the Ketubah has been preserved. It proves that in spite of all the vicissitudes through which the Jewish people have passed, in spite of their dispersion into every corner of the earth they have yet maintained unbroken their religious and legal unity. They were swayed by one and the same tradition. They submitted to the same legal prescriptions. They knew that by so doing they would preserve the sanctity and morality of their marriage, the purity of their home life and the real protection for their women and children. Hence it has come that wherever such a Jewish marriage has been performed and the parties possess a Ketubah, it has been recognized and respected whithersoever husband and wife have gone, and has entitled them to the right of forming part of the Jewish Community wherever such existed.

Proceeding from the inner form to the outer the Ketubah possesses additional features of no mean importance. The writing itself is of extreme value. Jewish Calligraphy is almost an unknown art, for no one has yet paid attention to it, while the science Jewish Palæography is in its earliest infancy if it has yet been born, which I doubt. In public and private libraries there exist some thousands of Hebrew MSS. gathered from all parts of the world, some very old, others more recent. Numerous catalogues have appeared in which these MSS. are briefly described, and here and there, especially in the catalogues of Oxford and the British Museum, some specimens have been added. But hitherto, all that the authors of these catalogues have been able to do is merely to divide in a rather rough and ready manner, those MSS. which were written in the East and those which were written in the West, in the latter case with some minor classification whether of Italian, Franco-German or Spanish type. No one, however, has yet undertaken any real investigation on the lines of Greek or Latin Palæography.

It must also be remembered that a large number of these Hebrew MSS. have no date. It is no easy task to determine the year or even the century in which such MSS. have been written, and so the authors of the catalogues were satisfied with mere guesswork. The absence of dates is the real drawback in determining the value of a MS. from the palæographical point of view. Then, we have square writing, so called Rashi writing and cursive writing, and between all these there are also intermediate forms. That is as far as the calligraphy goes and therefore, as remarked above, when it comes to the fixing of the age of a manuscript or a document which has otherwise no definite date, we are left to wild conjecture.

It is a peculiar feature of Hebrew Calligraphy that the character of the various forms of writing, square or cursive, the Majuscule or Minuscule, often remains unchanged for centuries. Recent discoveries of old documents in the Genizah have taught Jewish scholars the wholesome lesson not to try and fix the date by the mere character of the script, although a very careful examination reveals slight changes which develop in the course of time and which it is the science of Palæography to trace. The unchanged character of Hebrew script is best seen in the scrolls of the Law. Except for some very definite differences between Sephardic and Ashkenazic, some of the latter being of an artificial character, it would be very difficult for any one at a mere glance to determine the age of such a scroll, so closely does one scribe follow the technique of an older scribe, and train himself as much as possible to imitate the older example. And yet even here differences can be detected. How can they be fixed? The vast material of the Ketubah, hailing from every part of the world and continuing through the Ages, can alone form the one solid basis upon which the study of Hebrew Calligraphy and Palæography can be reared.

The two fundamental conditions for a scientific investigation of this branch of study are time and place. It is essential to be able to state the exact time when a ducument is written, and the exact place where it has been written. These are definite starting points, and these two essentials the Ketubah alone can offer. As mentioned before, the very starting point of the Ketubah is the accurate date and the minute description of the place. It often happens that even when a Hebrew manuscript is dated, the place of writing is not mentioned, and one is left to mere guesswork; sometimes later copyists embody the original date when transcribing the old original, for that date may be the very year of the composition. Thus a date found at the end of a MS., instead of helping to determine the time and place of writing, becomes misleading. In the same way the only satisfactory means of determining the character of the script, to which country or age it belongs, what hand it may be, oriental or occidental, Spanish or Italian, Syrian or Egyptian, can only be by the study of the Ketubah.

The writers are, as a rule, professional scribes; the writing is very carefully done, at least as carefully and beautifully as any MS. and in fact often clearer and better. Much more depends upon a Ketubah being clearly written than upon a MS. The consequences in the one case can be very serious if an important word has been left out, and may vitiate the whole contract, whilst a word omitted or carelessly written in a MS. can only create a slight difficulty in the understanding, and this can be rectified by comparing one MS. with another copy of it. Not so the Ketubah which is quite individual in character. No comparison can help. In addition, corrections or erasures are not allowed in a Ketubah, and when any correction is made between the lines, this fact must be specially noted at the bottom of the document and signed by witnesses. We have thus in the Ketubah the best specimens of Hebrew Calligraphy, and it is only necessary to collect them and group them according to time and place, to obtain a well documented and fully authenticated history of Jewish writing throughout the ages.*) Besides, we would have in these Ketubot some excellent specimens of Jewish penmanship and indirectly again an indication of the economic conditions of the time and of the social status of the parties concerned.

The well-being or the poverty of the people is also reflected in the shape of the document and in the material used for the Ketubah. The Ketubot of the poor people fleeing from the pogroms in Russia are small crunched up little bits of paper with irregular writing, carelessly handled and often almost illegible. Documents hailing from Spain, Italy and the East are superb leaves of parchment, of a large size, well dressed, a delight to the eye, a thorough æsthetical pleasure, and not a few of them also monuments of art, as shown by the specimens here published.

*) From the few specimens published here, the reader will be able to see at a glance, how individualistic the writing of the Ketubah really is and how clearly these represent the types and forms which Hebrew writing has assumed in various parts and through various ages. Thus Plate II, the headpiece from Fostat, represents the very characteristic oriental writing, probably of the 12th century. It consists of a fragment of the introductory poem, whilst Plate III gives us a specimen of the more cursive writing of the text current among the Egyptian Jews of the 11th or 12th century. On the other hand the text of the Ketubah of Krems, Plate VII, is Western (Ashkenasic) square writing, while Plate IV is a specimen of cursive Spanish writing of the 19th century. Again, that of Ancona, Plate I, is square as well as cursive Italian writing of the 18th century. Close upon 1000 years separate the one from the other, and yet they allow us to see the similarities and changes which have grown up in the course of that time and give us the means for establishing Jewish Palæography on a scientific basis.

Especial interest has recently arisen in Jewish Art. A few investigations have been carried out dealing with illuminated Hebrew Books and MSS. We are here again merely on the threshold, and much of the work done is, with few exceptions, of a dilettante character. No comparative studies have been made, nor any search for the origin. It is naturally to be presumed that the Princes of Exile, following the example of other great and exalted personages, may have indulged in such a luxury as an illuminated Bible, or some rich man in that of an illuminated Haggadah for Passover. But unfortunately we are moving in the domain of mere guesswork. Few specimens of old work have thus far been discovered and treated, and the old problem of the Jewish painters and artists is still a work for the future.

It would be interesting to find out whether there was a school of Jewish painters or illuminators, considering that not a few illuminated MSS. have been preserved, in spite of the ravages of time and the usual danger of destruction to which beautiful works of art are always exposed. They have always formed the first portion of loot and were the more easily destroyed. It was their beauty which was their doom.

There must have been, especially in Italy and Spain, a good many Jewish artists, for a Hebrew treatise on illumination has been preserved in the library of Parma. But here, so far, very little has been done. A vast field lies before the student of Jewish Art if he only know where to go. Of course, the student who wishes to study such MSS. would have to face the same difficulties, to some extent, as the man who wishes to determine the place and age of an undated MS. Not only are the names of the illuminators not known, but neither has there been preserved the name of any Jewish Mæcenas who could have paid for such a handsome and beautiful illuminated

MS. It is almost paradoxical, however, to mention that one of the Medicis seems to have been the patron of Jewish art, for many years ago, I discovered a beautifully illuminated Hebrew MS. in the library of Turin, dedicated to one of that family, if my memory be correct. The name of an illuminator was given on the title page of that MS. in the shape of musical notes, which I was able to read as Fa. Re. Sol. La., no doubt the famous Farisol, known as the beautiful scribe as well as an author.

Thus far only a few illuminated Bibles have come down to us; those in my possession have been published by me, while specimens of others, notably from the Petersburg library, by Gunzburg and Stassoff, but these works are now practically inaccessible. A few more illuminated Bibles are known to exist like the Farchi, now Sassoon, Bible and its counterpart formerly Loewe, and the Kennicott Bible in Oxford. Other illuminations are found in Service Books, prayer books of all kinds. Then the Passover service, the Haggadah, and the scroll of Esther were sometimes illuminated. But taking them all together the number of such illuminated monuments is very small. It took a long time to write and illuminate a whole MS. Incomparably richer, however, is the yield of the Ketubot. These were not merely legal formularies but living evidence of the joyful occasion. Everything connected with the marriage had to bear a joyous appearance and nothing that could embellish the occasion could be neglected. The result was that care was taken to make that document at least as beautiful as a page of the Haggadah, an illuminated title page or inside page of a prayer book. For at least as much care was taken in the writing of the Ketubah as in the writing of the other documents. We find, therefore, the Ketubah often set within an ornamental frame, surrounded on all sides with various kinds of illustrations, flowers, symbolical signs, fishes, acorns, and all the other details found in illuminated manuscripts.

This then is genuine Jewish art, being sometimes of a very high order; at others, simple forms showing signs of decay or the work of second and third rate artists. But even in its decadent form, it still bears the traces of finer models. Any one bent on the study of Jewish art would thus find in the large number of Ketubot an inexhaustible mine for investigation. The changes, to which reference has been made, of time, country, Minhag etc, were sure to show themselves as well in the varying schools of artists called upon to illuminate these Ketubot. One would then be able, at the hand of these witnesses, to discuss the problem of Schools of Art and of Artists' Guilds, and to find perhaps that the Hebrew family titles of Sebuim and Edomim were nothing but the names of the guilds of illuminators and painters of miniatures, the Dei Tintor and Dei Rossi. It must be remembered that the name of "miniature" is derived from the red "minium" used for these small paintings, and the word Edomim would be almost a literal translation of "Miniaturist", the man who used the "Red Minium". It is a fascinating subject but no one has yet turned his attention to these beautiful illustrations. Even down to the beginning of the last century the Ketubah issued by the Bevis Marks Synagogue here in London had an illustrated border with symbolical figures. These were already copperplate engravings, but they preserved the ancient tradition, now entirely done away with. Many a symbolical figure has often been painted on such Ketubot. Quaint no doubt, but suggestive: such as the picture of the constellation of Pisces which is the symbol of fruitfulness and at the same time a kind of charm against the evil eye (see Plate I). In another Ketubah in my possession which is reproduced here, in full but on a greatly reduced scale (see Plate VI), the bride's name being Esther and the wedding taking place in the month of Adar, was sufficient reason for the artist to make the frame of interlaced geometrical figures and other symetrical drawings from the whole of the scroll of Esther written minutely and yet extraordinarily clearly.

It resembles the interlaced marginal Massorah written in a similar manner round the oldest codices of the Bible, masterpieces of Jewish penmanship and highly valuable specimens of Micrography. In between the empty spaces there are stars, flowers and gold studs; the constellation of the month of Adar and other symbolical figures, as well as incidents in the Biblical history referring to the marriage, are painted in the corners of the Ketubah. It is the work of an Italian artist who lived in Rome.*)

It would be easy to multiply examples of such artistic work which, by the fact that all these illustrations have been circumscribed by time and place, can easily be fixed chronologically. Such Ketubot offer most reliable and invaluable information on the history of Jewish Art.

One last word. It was customary among Jews and Gentiles to write an Epithalamium, a kind of rhymed poem in honour of bride and bridegroom, and to offer one's good wishes for the future happiness of the young couple. Even that bare legal document had to be at the

*) Unfortunately the exigencies of printing demanded a great reduction in the size of the print. In consequence, the minute writing escapes the naked eye. It may also be noticed that the bride and bridegroom (see plate V) and the other people appearing in the Ketubah are dressed in Empire costume. In the Leipzig prayer-book of the 14th century (see page 9) as well as in the Haggadah of Nuremberg of the 15th century (see page 54) the bridal pair appear in the usual mediæval costume. In the fragmentary Ketubah from Krems of 1392 the bridegroom wears the *Judenhut* and carries in his hand the well-known wedding ring, of which a few specimens still survive.

same time the bearer of good wishes for future happiness and prosperity, and symbolical verses, metaphorical interpretations of Scripture texts, together with good wishes, were therefore added to the Ketubah. They form a kind of poetical and symbolical introduction, a primitive form of Epithalamium, and no doubt often the starting point of such poems as can still be found among the writings of Jewish poets.

In summing up, there is scarcely a single chapter of Jewish life which is not directly or indirectly touched upon in the Ketubah. In many instances it is the only source of information that we possess. It helps us to draw up a reliable map of the Jewish dispersion. It assists us in reconstructing the appearance and disappearance of Jewish communities. It helps us to trace generation after generation. It is the only source from which we can discover the mothers in Israel and thus throw a new light upon the forces which moulded the characters of our great men and lifted them to the highest pinnacle of erudition or state-craft, of success or failure, in the walks of life in which they trod. The Ketubah opens the door to the inner chamber. We have a peep into the wardrobe of the bride, and we are able to estimate the financial worth of the rich men of old. The social and economic conditions of life stand clearly revealed, the value of the currency we are able to estimate. The historical background, which explains new conditions imposed upon the husband, opens up a vista of uncertainty, of danger and of trouble. We learn to appreciate Jewish penmanship, and we find a new basis for the study of reliable Palæography.

And as for Jewish Art, a new treasure house is found in the Ketubah.

And now having finished it seems quite obvious: it was only necessary to point it out. But, having done so, I press that the immediate collection, examination and preservation of all available Ketubot be undertaken whereever possible: that special archives be established for the safe keeping of these invaluable documents, and that photographic reproductions of the oldest specimens be made available to all students of Jewish history. It is without doubt the most fascinating and romantic chapter in the history of Jewish civilization.

WEDDING CEREMONY.
From an illuminated Haggadah of the XVth Century,
Nuremberg National Museum.

PLATES

KETUBAH OF ANCONA, 1776
Cod. Gaster, 1658.

PLATE I

FRAGMENT OF A KETUBAH FROM FOSTAT, X—XIth CENTURY
Bodleian Library, Cod. 2807. Heb. c. 13.
By kind permission of the Bodleian Library.

PLATE II

FRAGMENT OF A KETUBAH FROM FOSTAT, X—XIth CENTURY
Bodleian Library, Cod. 2807. Ms. Heb. c. 13. By kind permission of the Bodleian Library.

PLATE III

KETUBAH OF GIBRALTAR, 1811
Cod. Gaster, 1662.

PLATE IV

NUPTIAL PAIR
DETAIL FROM A KETUBAH OF ROME, 1818
Cod. Gaster, 1677.

PLATE V

KETUBAH OF ROME, 1818
Cod. Gaster, 1677.

PLATE VI

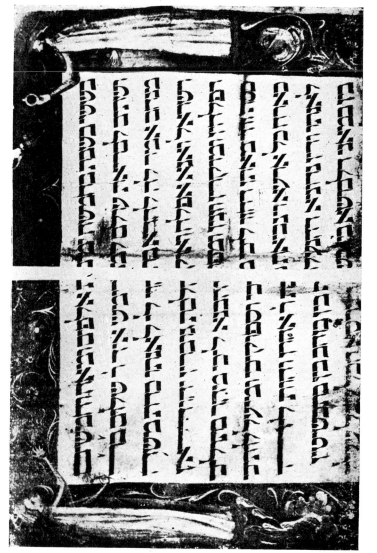

KETUBAH OF KREMS, 1392.
Vienna Hofbibliothek, Cod. Hebr. 218.
From "Archiv für jüdische Familienforschung", Vienna 1913.

PLATE VII

DETAIL FROM A KETUBAH OF RIVAROLO, 1727
Collection of the Jewish Community in Berlin.

PLATE VIII

PLATE IX

Ferrara, Italy, 5387 Anno Mundi (1627 C. E.)
Parchment, black on white 13¾ x 20 in. (35x51 cm)

Bridegroom: Moses, son of Jacob Mi-Napoli (Di Napoli)
Bride: Bella Fior, divorcee, daughter of Raphael Mi-Castello
(Castelli)

A rectangular border formed by Psalm CXXVIII written in bold letters is surrounded by a double frame of appropriate micrographic texts from Isaiah (LXI,
9-12 and LXII, 1-9) and Psalms (XLV and I, 3). The innermost border is formed by
Proverbs XXXI, 10-31 written in micrography. The crown above the text is inscribed: "The crown of good name surpasses them all" (Aboth IV, 12).

An elegant but simple design lacking the artistic devices of the typical Italian
Ketuboth. The absence of all representation of human form is an indication of
strong puritanical tendencies and it may represent a continuation of the style of
Hebrew illuminated Bibles of Muslim Spain. The frame formed by multiple
lines of script of varying sizes bears a striking resemblance to that of Folio 310 in
the Damascus Keter (Burgos, Spain, 1260).

LIBRARY OF THE JEWISH THEOLOGICAL SEMINARY OF AMERICA,
NEW YORK.

שיר המעלות אשרי כל ירא יי׳ ההלך בדרכיו יגע

בית והון נחלת אבות ומי׳ אשה משכלת

בגמטא

PLATE X

Mantua, Italy. 5397 A. M. (1636 C. E.)
Parchment, colors. 19x25 in. (48x63 cm)

Bridegroom: Jacob, son of Kalonymos Me-Italia (Da Italia)
Bride: Beracha, daughter of the illustrious scholar, Samuel
    Meldola, the Physician

Scrolls inscribed with Psalm CXXVIII spiral around a pair of twin columns
which form a portal. The inscriptions in the two panels above the columns
allude to the names of the bride and the groom. An idealized view of Jerusalem
appears in the entablature, topped by a crude representation of Mount Zion.
The finials are inscribed with the opening words of a quote from Jeremiah
XXXIII, 11 with the closing words appearing on the bases of the columns. The
area formed by the archway is filled with a double coat of arms presumably
combining the crests of the two families as it is inscribed with the words "both
shall be as one" (Eccl. XI, 6).

The massive portal with the heavy entablature, the pair of corpulent angels,
bosomy cherubs, birds and squirrels are features characteristic of a typical
baroque ketubah.

Genealogical Note

Rabbi Samuel Meldola, scion of a long line of rabbis and physicians was a noted
author and court physician of the Duke of Mantua. His descendants include
Raphael Meldola (1754-1828), author and rabbi of the Sephardim of London.

The *Da'Italia* family was the founder of a printing press in Mantua in 1612.

LIBRARY OF THE JEWISH THEOLOGICAL SEMINARY OF AMERICA,
NEW YORK.

PLATE XI

Verona, Italy. 5455 A.M. (1695 C. E.)
Parchment, colors. 20x34 in. (51x86 cm)

Bridegroom: Solomon Hai, son of Jonah Scandiano
Bride: Leah, daughter of the late Raphael Moses Segal Morteira
Witnesses: Mordecai, son of Samuel Hayyim Basan
            Nathan Hayyim, son of Samuel Ashkenazi

No less than 42 vignettes and medallions decorate this ketubah which is also adorned with grape-laden vines and flowers, birds and fish, fountains and angels, all centered around the ubiquitous representation of Jerusalem. The six medallions suspended from the vines depict the happiness of family life as expressed in Psalms CXXVIII. The double miniatures framing the text represent the twelve Tribes of Israel and the twelve signs of the Zodiac. The miniatures alternate with medallions containing biblical scenes related to the four elements (top and bottom), the five senses (right and left and top left corner) and the four seasons (the four corners with the top left corner serving in a double capacity).

It is peculiar that while the zodiacal symbols are arranged counterclockwise with those of the months of Ab and Ellul (Leo and Virgo) transposed, the symbols of the twelve Tribes are placed clockwise and are grouped according to their journey in the Wilderness (cf. Numbers X). The name of Dan appears twice, once replacing Gad.

This extravagantly rich design enjoyed great popularity in the last third of the seventeenth century. This is one of several surviving specimens with identical design. Others known are from Padua, 1670 and 1696, Mantua, 1696 and Venice, 1677.

Genealogical Note

The *Morteira* family counted among its members a number of scholars, the most renowned being Rabbi Saul Halevi M., Rabbi of Amsterdam (1560-1660).

Rabbi Mordecai Basan (Bassani) of Verona, an important rabbinical scholar and author, was the great-grandfather of Menahem Navarra (cf. Cecil Roth, *Gleanings*, p. 203)

LIBRARY OF THE JEWISH THEOLOGICAL SEMINARY OF AMERICA, NEW YORK.

בששי בשבת עשרה ימים לחדש מנחם שנת חמשת, אלפים וארבע מאות חמשים וחמשה
לבריאת העולם למנין שאנו מנין בו פ ויניזיא מתא דיתבא על נהר אדיע נא הבחור ויזכר
כבר שלזלכר חיי זעזה בחר יוזר מר וי אן יד זאמר לי בתורה העניע זחיי זונה מרת
לאה בתזירלא לקח נת הבזון במרחה ואלך מ' ז, ג, בי רובינרה זלהא הוי לי לאנתו כרית
משה וישראל ואנא בסי על שמה דא שמרה ואוקיר ואיזן ואפלנס יתיכי וחלכא גובין יוראין
רקיון וזוקרין וזזן וכפרנסין לנשיהון בקו דנא ויהיבנא ליב רהר בתזירלא כסף זוז דחזו
ליבי וזונך וכסותיך וסיפוקיך ומיעלך לותיכי כאורח כל אריא ויצבאת קרת לאה בתזירלא רצא
הלא והות ליה לאנתו ודין גדוניא דהנעלת ליה מבי אבוה בין בכסף בין בדהב בין בתכשיטין
ארבע מאות וחמשים זיקאטי בכל זך וייעת לוישבעב ליעד שיטא טרוע ואיביע מקדמי לא מזבע
קומיליך הלבשא, יעד שלזל מאית דינרא בכל זך כנים עליניה ותוסאיטב דהייני מזביל השינכע
רוז הבלה כבת הכל וצב כלכ שלזזה זי יה חתן יצ, חתן דנן ואוסף זה להזדיליה עשרין למאא הך הכר
הכל על מקוקב כורך רבוני זדב ודהב זהזכב לי זעי רבבא זך הכל כתובתא גדוניא ותוספא
תשע מאות דיזקאני ליעד רוני וכר אמר שלזה הי יע חתן דנן אחריות כתובתא רא וא קבלית
עלי על יה בחין אי להזאריע מן כל שתר וא נכסן וקנין וקי דאיה לי בתת כל שמיא דקנאיואבת
רא עיד נמיה ואפילו מן גלימא הל כתפאי בחי ובזירא מן יומא דנן ולעלם וכבל עלי כך שלזה
העניע ויהביזויה וחומריה דנא אסמכתא ולא בטוטפסי רשטרי וקינא אנן שהרי דה העיל לתהא מן
כבי יצ חתן דנן יע, צה חתן דנן לזוכית מרת לאה בתורלתא רא חמא יעל כל מאי דכתיב
וכפרש לעיל במנא דכשר למקנא ביה והכל שרירוקים

שלזה הי יע זהי שגדי כתובתא רא

בר שלזל יע זהי שגד כתובתא רא

PLATE XII

Ferrara, Italy. 5479 A. M. (1719 C.E.)
Parchment, colors. 24x30 in. (61x76 cm)

Bridegroom: Joseph Baruch, son of Menahem Rocas
Bride: Diamante, daughter of Samuel Halevi
Witnesses: Mordecai, son of Jacob Zahalon
Shabbetai Elhanan, son of Judah Raphael Hayyim
Recanati

The ornamentation of this early 18th century ketubah represents a curious blend of genuine Jewish elements and stylistic motifs borrowed from the secular environment. The undulated top is resplendent with peacocks, flowers and floating cherubs flanked by the bridal couple in the formal costumes of the period including the flowing *parucca* of the bridegroom and the *decolletage* of the bridal gown.

The grape vine, the olive branch and the rose bough held out in the hands of the cherubs, are appropriately inscribed with, respectively, Song of Songs VII, 13, Psalms CXXVIII, 3 and Song of Songs II, 2.

The tapestry-like border with its dainty floral scroll work is embellished with six medallions containing, counterclockwise, the following scenes: Abraham welcoming the three angels, with Sarah in the background; Esther received by King Ahasuerus; Rachel and Leah meeting with Jacob; Isaac meeting Rebecca; Mordecai on horseback led by Haman; Adam and Eve in the Garden of Eden. The inscription on the outer border reads: "In a good sign and in good luck to the bridegroom and the bride and to the entire house of Israel." "The Lord make the woman that is come to thy house like Rachel and like Leah which did build" (*sic!*) (Ruth IV, 11)

Genealogical Note

Mordecai Zahalon (?-1748), Physician and Rabbi of Ferrara, was a talented Hebrew poet and author of several rabbinic works.

Shabbetai Elhanan Recanati, scion of an old Italian family of rabbis and kabbalists, was the rabbi of the Spanish community of Ferrara. His responsa and halakic decisions are incorporated in Lampronti's *Pahad Yizhak* and in the works of other contemporary rabbinic authors.

COLLECTION OF MR. BERNARD ZUCKER, NEW YORK

PLATE XIII

Reggio (Emilia), Italy. 5534 A.M. (1774 C.E.)
Parchment, black and ocher. 17 x 22 in. (43x56 cm)

Bridegroom: Jacob, son of Joshua Levi
Bride: Abishag, daughter of Israel Mi'Zekenim
Witnesses: Israel, son of Isaiah Bassan
Samson Hayyim, son of Nahman Michael Nahmani

The intricate design of this ketubah is made up entirely of texts in six different sizes of calligraphy. The geometric patterns formed by these texts are reminiscent of decorated Hebrew manuscripts from 15th century Portugal. The use of this austere style in the late 18th century indicates the existence in Italy of a Sephardic tradition of manuscript decoration alongside a dominant trend of richer ornamentation. (Cf. Plate IX)

The texts are from Proverbs XXXI, Ruth IV, 11, and Song of Songs. Flower vases, fleurs-de-lis, and other floral motifs as well as Stars-of-David were stamped with metal dies in all available space - a step toward the mechanical production of decorative ketubot.

Genealogical Note

The Mi'Zekenim (Del Vecchi), as its name indicates, was one of the ancient Italian Jewish families.

Rabbi Israel (Benjamin) Bassan (Bassani) (1703-1790), son of the renowned Rabbi Isaiah Bassani who was the teacher of Rabbi Moses Hayyim Luzzato, was himself a rabbinic author and a skilful poet both in Hebrew and Italian. Giorgio Bassani, the popular Italian novelist is probably a descendant of this old rabbinic family.

Samson Hayyim Nahmani (?-1779), Rabbi of Siena and Reggio, was a kabbalist and a prolific author of rabbinic works. (Cf. *Jewish Encyclopedia* vol. IX, p. 144, where his father's name is wrongly given as Nahman *Raphael.*)

THE NEW YORK PUBLIC LIBRARY, JEWISH DIVISION

PLATE XIV

Reggio (Emilia), Italy. 5555 A. M. (1774 C. E.)
Parchment, gold and colors. 15½x19 in. (39½x41½ cm)

Bridegroom: Abraham Mazal Tov, son of Zechariah Fontanella
Bride: Gentille, daughter of the great luminary . . . . the il-
lustrious Rabbi Isaiah Carmi
Witnesses: Eliakum, son of Abraham Padovani
Abiad, son of Ishmael Leone

There is nothing Jewish in the charmingly decorated border of this ketubah save
for the Hebrew inscriptions on the four drapes and on the two tablatures. The
cherubs, mermaids, birds and kissing doves as well as the coronet and the cornucopia are all standard stylistic features of late eighteenth century rococo ornamentation. Presumably, the artist was a non-Jew.

Genealogical Note

The bridegroom was a relative, possibly a grandson, of Rabbi Israel Berachya
Fontanella of Reggio whose approbation appears on the *Todat Shelamim*
(Venice, 1740)

The father of the bride, *Rabbi Isaiah Carmi* the head of the talmudic academy in
Reggio and a noted poet, was a pupil and successor in the rabbinate to Rabbi
Israel Benjamin Bassani (see Plate XII.) One of his kinsmen, Jacob Israel Carmi,
represented Italian Jewry at Napoleon's Sanhedrin (1806).

THE NEW YORK PUBLIC LIBRARY, JEWISH DIVISION

בס"ד

וישמח מאשת נעוריך

יהי מקורך ברוך

בסימנא טבא ובמזלא מעליא

ברביעי בשבת שלשה עשר יום לחדש אב שנת חמשת אלפים וחמש מאות וחמשים
וחמש לבריאת העולם למנין שאנו מנין פה רינגייו מתא דיתבא על נהר פו וסמוך לחד מיא ת
בא הבחור המפואר וריקך כמהר אברהם מזל טוב בן מנוחת המרומם כמהר ... כ ...
פינטאנילה זלהה ואמר לה להרא בתולתא הצנועה המהוללה ומשכלת מרת ... נ ... ז ... ר ...
מבחרת המאור והגדול מעזי הגדול ומרדכי הרב המופלא כמוהרר שעיה הן קמי נ ... ד ר ...
לאנת כרו ... משה וישראל ואנא בסר אפלחה ואוקיר ואזן ואפרנס ... אנשיהו ... כ ...
כורין יהודאי דפלחין ומוקרין וזנין וי ... פרנסין ומכסין ... נשיהון בקושטא ... ה ...
ליכי מהר ... ליכי כסף זוזי מתנן חזו ליכי ונ ... וכס ... כי ... ו ... ל ...
כ ... ו ... מ ... מ ... מת ...
ו ... ע ... ה ... ליטרין של כסף ... ל ... א ...
וחזר ... ליטרין של כסף צרוף נמצא ס ... כ ...
בין ... ו ... ארבעין ... של כסף ... ו ... ר ... ה ... ו ...
ל ... א ... ט ... ח ... ד ... ש ... נ ...
ו ... קבילית עלי ... דתהא להתפרעא מכל ... ק ... נ ... כ ... ו ...
ד ... כל ... ש ... נכסי ... ר ... א ... ל ...
דל ... א ... כ ... ו ... ל ... ב ... מ ...
כתובתא ... ו ... ו ... ג ... ע ... כ ... ו ... ח ... מ ...
רן ... א ... ו ... ש ... כ ... נ ... ו ... נ ... ו ...
אברהם מזל טוב ... ח ... ו ... כ ... ש ... נ ... ד ... ב ...
ישראל הצ ... ו ... ה ... ה ... כ ... ל ... כ ... ל ...
כ ... ו ... ה ... ד ... כ ... א ... א ...
מזל טוב ... כ ... פינטאנילה זלהה ... ר ... ל ...
הכבודה ... ה ... נ ... ה ... ב ... כ ... ש ... ר ... ק ...
מ ... ע ... כ ... פ ... ל ... מ ... ש ... ט ...

יחזו ... יראו בבניך

יפרו וירמו כרעננים

PLATE XV

Bosetto, Italy. 5561 A. M. (1801 C. E.)
Parchment, black on white. 19½x23in. (49½x58½ cm)

Bridegroom: Isaac Samuel, son of Raphael Solomon Halevi
Bride: Sarah, daughter of Zechariah David Fontanella

The twelve vignettes forming the border are pen-and-ink drawings of the Zodiac. The only other decorative elements of this ketubah are the hand pouring water from a pitcher (symbol of the Levi family) above the text, and a dove with an olive branch in its beak (presumably the birde's family crest), below. The twelve panels are interspaced with appropriate quotes from Proverbs XVIII, 28. and Jeremiah XXX,I 11. Note the peculiar lettering of the inscriptions with the exaggerated ascenders of the *lamed.*

As is the case with the earlier illuminated ketuboth (cf. Plate XI), the zodiacal symbols are arranged in an irregular sequence with Virgo (Ellul) preceding Libra (Tishre) and Gemini (Sivan) preceding Aries (Nisan).

Especially intriguing are the between-the-line substitutions appearing over the crossed out original date and names. The thus inserted date is 5620 (1860), i.e. fifty-nine years after the original date.The family name of the bridegroom has been left unchanged. Presumably, the text of the old ketubah was being used as a guide by the scribe of a later generation who, as a precaution, inserted the new data lest he copy the old text with names and date. Possibly, the new bridegroom was a grandson of the old, both being of the Halevi family.

THE NEW YORK PUBLIC LIBRARY, JEWISH DIVISION

שטח : אשה : רטים : קשת : גדי : דלי : מצא

לצחק : חנה :

עקרב

תאומים

בתולה

טלה

מאזנים

טוב : אריה : שמאל : סרטן : קטן : שור : מצא

PLATE XVI

Pitiliano, Italy. 5604 A.M. (1843 C. E.)
Parchment, black on white.

Bridegroom: Abraham, son of Menahem of Lapergola
Bride: Malka, daughter of Solomon Nehemiah Servi

This ketubah represents in more than one respect the spiritual and material decline of Italian Jewry in the nineteenth century. Its frugal design is adorned by a solitary vignette showing Abraham's sacrifice of Isaac (an allusion to the bridegroom's name) and by the following inscriptions in bold script: "In a good sign and in good luck to the bridegroom and the bride" (top); "The voice of joy and the voice of gladness, the voice of the bridegroom and voice of the bride" (Jer. XXXIII, 11. - right and left corners); "And Abraham shall surely become a great and mighty nation" (Gen. XXXVIII, 18. - right); "And God Almighty give you mercy before the man" (Gen. XLIM, 14. - left) - a rather ominous adhortation to a bride . . . .

Wrong Date

The full date in this ketubah is given as Sunday, the fourteenth day of Tishre, in the year Six-Thousand-and-Four, Anno Mundi. This would put the marriage as having taken place in the year 2244 C.E.! The actual year, however, must have been 5604 (1843 C. E.) as the ketubah refers to a civil marriage agreement executed on September 20, 1843. Indeed, the fourteenth day of Tishre in 1843 was Sunday. This colossal mistake, which possibly invalidated the ketubah, is a telling sign of the poor qualifications of the religious functionary who had performed the marriage. Such error would have been unthinkable in previous generations of Italian Jewry.

Who was the ignorant marriage-performer? We shall never know. The ketubah is mutilated with the signatures of the witnesses - generally the learned of the community - missing. . . .

COLLECTION OF MR. BERNARD ZUCKER, NEW YORK

בסימנא טבא

ובמזלא מעליא לחתנא ולכלתא

א ב

קול ששון וקול שמחה קול חתן וקול כלה

באחד בשבת יום ארבעה עשר לחדש חשון שנת חמשת אלפים ותרכ"א לבריאת ה' עלם למנין שאנו
מנין פה פיטיגליאנו יושבה על ארעא דיתבא על נ'... לינערי מליינ... ופיקי' בא לפנינו הבחור הכפאר
כמר אברהם בן ה- יקר והנכבד כבוד מהרה מלאפינצא... כ' יען תאמר להדא בתולתא הכבודה הצנועה מרית
שלמה בת חיק מההר - חנני... כמל מה גב שרי צפטין... לאננו בית משה רישר ואנא אפלח ואוקיר...

ואזון ואפרנס ואסה יתכי כהלכת גוברין יהודאין דפלחין ומוקרין וזנין ומפרנסין לנשיהון בקושטא ויהיבנא ליכי
מוהר בתוליכי מאה זוז... ... רחמי רחיז ליב מראוריתא... ... ... ויצבי ... רותיכ מרית מאה כל ארעא וצבא
מיך מלכה כלותא... בתולתא... ... ... לכבר אברהם... ... ... דהנעלת ליה מבי... מזה קך
... ... נטריר של יום עשרים
... ... וצבי היקר כמר אברהם ... ... עשרים סקורדי למאה
כל ... ... מלבר כסף זהי מאתן וחצי לה
כל יכי ... ... רא קבילת על ועל יוסי
... ... רה
... ... בן
... ... אברהם יצו
... ... ורלא
... ...
... ...

צו לבבה וככריה בתולתא מרית מלכה מבת בת היקר ... יצו תבנ ... יאי קן אס גנא כמשר
למקיים בנא בזה ורכל שריר וברור וקים

קול ששון וקול שמחה קול חתן וקול כלה

PLATE XVII

Belle Harbor, New York 5734 A. M. (1974 C. E.)
Imitation parchment, colors. 11¾ x 18½ in. (30x47 cm)

Bridegroom: Eliezer Alexander Zisskind, son of Shalom
Ha-Cohen
Bride: Bracha, daughter of Judah Ha-Cohen

The design of this contemporary American Ketubah is in more than one way representative of the eclecticism of American Jewish culture. Artistically, it is a blend of diverse styles, with elements both traditional and modern. The richness of its decor is a reflection of the affluence of the American Jewish community and of the lavishness of its weddings.

The outer border in the shape of a Moorish window is inscribed with a series of good omens, one for each letter of the alphabet. Similar inscriptions are found in some oriental ketubot. The inner border, in the form of a banner, is in Art Nouveau style recently revived from its *fin de siecle* popularity.

The space formed by the arc of the outer frame is filled with a dense commixture of traditional symbols: six-branched candelabrum supported by a pair of doves; richly ornamented crown topped by Star of David and flanked by the letters Aleph and Beth, the respective initials of the groom and the bride; scrolls inscribed with the words: "The voice of joy and the voice of gladness, the voice of the bridegroom and the voice of the bride." (Jer. XXXIII, 11)

The artistic balance is restored by the highly professional script of the text using a lucid and esthetically pleasing lettering style.

DESIGNED BY DUK ENGELHARDT OF REMBRANDT ASSOCIATES, NEW YORK

רביעי בשבת ארבעה ימים לחדש ניסן
שנת חמשת אלפים ושבע מאות ושלשים וארבע לבריאת
עולם למנין שאנו מנין כאן בעל הארבור, עו יורק איך
החתן אליעזר אלכסנדר זיסקינד בן שלום הכהן
אמר לה להדא בתולתא

⚜ ברכה בת יהודה הכהן ⚜

הוי לי לאנתו כדת משה וישראל ואנא אפלח ואוקיר ואיזון
ואפרנס יתיכי ליכי כהלכות גוברין יהודאין דפלחין ומוקרין וזנין
ומפרנסין לנשיהון בקושטא ויהבנא ליכי מוהר בתוליכי כסף זוזי
מאתן דחזי ליכי מדאורייתא ומזוניכי וכסותיכי וסיפוקיכי ומיעל לותיכי
כאורח כל ארעא וצביאת מרת ברכה בתולתא בחולתא
דא והות ליה לאנתו ודן נדוניא דהנעלת ליה מבי אבוה בין בכסף בין
ביהב בין בתכשיטין במאני דלבושא בשימושי דירה וב שימושא
דערסא הכל קבל עליו אליעזר אלכסנדר זיסקינד חתן דנן בלגאה
זקוקים כסף צריף וצבי אליעזר אלכסנדר זיסקים חתן דנן והוסיף לה
מן דיליה עוד מאה זקוקים כסף צריף אחרים כנגדן סך הכל
מאתים זקוקים כסף צריף וכך אמר אליעזר אלכסנדר זיסקינד חתן דנן
אחריות שטר כתובתא דא נדוניא דא ותוספתא דא קבלית עלי ועל
ירתי בתראי להתפרע מכל שפר ארג נכסין וקנינין דאית לי תחות כל
שמיא דקנאי ודעתיד אנא למיקנא נכסין דאית להון אחריות ודלית
להון אחריות כלהון יהון אחראין וערבאין לפרוע מנהון שטר כתובתא
דא נדוניא דן ותוספתא דא מנאי ואפילו מן גלימא דעל כתפאי בחיי
ובתר חיי מן יומא דנן ולעלם ואחריות וחומר שטר כתובתא דא נדוניא
דן ותוספתא דא קבל עליו אליעזר אלכסנדר זיסקינד חתן דנן כחומר כל
שטרי כתובות וחוספתות דנהגין בבנת ישראל העשויין כתיקון חכמינו
ז"ל דלא כאסמכתא ודלא כטופסי דשטרי **בן אליעזר אלכסנדר**

חתן דנן לעיל **ברכה בת יהודה הכהן** בתולתא דא על כל זה
דכהן ולפרש לעיל במנא דכשר למיקנא ביה הכל שריר וקים

_____ נאום

_____ נאום

NOTES

NOTES

NOTES

NOTES

NOTES